Break Free from Stillness

Mary W. Jensen

Briarbook Lane Press

BREAK FREE FROM STILLNESS by Mary W. Jensen

ISBN: 978-1-7376437-4-6

Published by Briarbook Lane Press

https://www.briarbooklane.com/

Cover and interior design by Mary W. Jensen

https://marywjensen.com/

https://www.briarbooklane.com/newsletter

A previous version of this collection was selected as a Quarterfinalist for the 2016 Mary Ballard Poetry Chapbook Prize.

Contents

Introduction

Dance is energy,
movement,
joy—
rhythm and flow.

Words pirouette on the page,
tap their way
across the keyboard.

In sync
with a body in motion,
never stale,
never still.

Who cares
what others think?

Dance alone,
or with a partner.

With a partner,
you must connect
and coordinate.

It falters
when steps fall
out of alignment.

Choose your partners carefully—
in love,
in business,
and in life.

Then step onto the floor.

The Music Begins

Unmoored

dandelion seed
freed from stems of the mundane,
dances in the wind

Music Beckons

Softly music begins to play;
I watch as others rise and dance,
content to simply watch
encased in shadow.

The music changes,
faster, more demanding.
To dance would be the fool...
but who will notice two tapping feet?

A drum starts a throb
my heart strives to match,
something stirs deep within
pulses energy through me.

Sway left, right.
Dare I join the dancers?

Release my inhibition,
surrender to the music,
spin, dip, laugh,
caring not what they think.

Dance to my own beat —
the music of my soul?

Tempo of Red

revitalizing cinnamon
a dozen illuminated candles
silk pajamas sliding under sheets
sweating in a sauna
heat of Mexico
rhythm of drums
flamenco, tango, pasodoble
cascading curtain of the stage
secret sonnets
serenades 'neath your balcony
fire cleansing old for new
sunset

Awaken

Take my hand
be still a moment
let your mind awaken
to splendor

do you hear it?
music surrounds you
in wind, traffic, laughter
sings harmony

energy connects
house and sky
man and earth
nothing stands alone

feel the crowd's rhythm
as it swirls around you
even now, as you pause,
the world is never still

light skips from one surface to the next
butterfly flits through air
laundry dances on clothesline
people pair off, hand in hand

colors blur as you dance
worry not about the steps
let your own soul guide you
I will lift you if you falter

taste the pleasure
as your body extends
the song on your tongue
sweet and fresh, yours alone

shape this power of music and movement
let your mind explore
your words dance
break free from stillness

In Flight

Muses of grace—airy butterflies
dance in pairs across the floor
in perfect meter.

A change in step, now vibrant birds —
rolling hips, compelling gaze,
seduce me.

My heart beats in rhythm,
yearns to dance as they —
be one with the music.

The Hold

Resonance

Rapt in your embrace,
my blood pulses music
in harmony with your own.

Sleep Long, Love

Dawn drifts through the curtain,
leaves shadows like lace
draped over your pale face.

I cherish the nights;
in sleep, the pain and worry fades
from your brow.

We can dream of better times:
the sunset on the ocean,
the moon over Paris;

You danced with me in Spain,
hiked the temples of Peru —
and now, the stairs are mountains.

I run my fingers gently
through your thinning dark hair,
wishing I could stay.

Though I must go, you are not alone —
the cat a dark shadow drapes over you,
lends warmth to chilled skin.

Sleep long and well, my Love.
When I return,
we'll cherish each moment.

Duet

We dance in harmony,
a daily waltz
to a song only we can hear.

Your hands on me,
breaths mingle,
steps slide into sync.

Your strength
to lift me
leaves me fearless.

Though one may step or turn away,
we never break hold—
partners for eternity.

The Dance

Dreams of music
dance through twilight,
soul offered in love.
Embrace
and spin
—Pause—
Spin and
embrace love
in offered soul.
Twilight through dance
music of dreams.

Form

The Ball

Arms up, back straight
follow his lead
body keeps form
mind roams free

Caress

Each word is a caress,
they make my skin glow.
My heart you do possess

Your novice poems impress,
the tempo nice and slow,
each word is a caress.

Our very breaths
join and banish woe.
My heart you do possess.

You don't say much, but less
is more, for I know
each word is a caress.

To your proposal I said yes,
a ring you did bestow;
my heart you do possess.

For with your first address
you had me at hello,
each word is a caress,
my heart you do possess.

Butterfly Sonnet

You once compared me to a butterfly —
A flitting soul unable to hold still,
A fragile silhouette against the sky;
Perhaps I even seem mentally ill.

Like insect on the wind seeking to moor,
Words tumble round trying to just break through;
A field of flowers are another lure,
Yet still I find my way back home to you.

But once I did not have these shiny wings,
A worm who had no confidence to fly.
Cocooned in your embrace I learned new things
My weaknesses are strengths in your mind's eye.

So even though I wander and I whine,
Believe me—I am yours and you are mine.

Courtship Song

A tale I sing of girl meets boy
He labored in her pa's employ
With wooden flute he played a tune
They danced beneath the Courtship Moon

They walked and talked, their love grew swift
One day he shared a precious gift
A golden pendant, meant to swoon
They danced beneath the Courtship Moon

A picnic meal down by the lake
Where he proposed her hand to take
With hearts that yearned to marry soon
They danced beneath the Courtship Moon

From out of darkness came a birth
And Moon looked down on Mother Earth
His heart engaged, he took a chance
As Earth and Moon resume their dance

With one full turn, from left to right
He courted her most every night
Then with a nod, they each advance
As Earth and Moon resume their dance

From birth, to marriage, then to death
Their love makes magic with each breath
An endless cycle of romance
As Earth and Moon resume their dance

Delight in Dance

Delight in dance; Muse play for me
a haunting song in one, two, three,
bestow grace to clumsy feet;
my steps cannot perform deceit,
body and soul in harmony.

Lyre plays on; my mate I see,
guide us to find unity
between our diverse beats;
Delight in dance.

Flow as water, we are free
to dance for eternity
as bodies meet and then retreat,
music makes me feel complete.
Muse, you inspire such jubilee,
Delight in dance.

A Turn

Musical Chairs

go
around
don't sit down
until music
STOPS

Do It Again

Another word, another page
Another day, another age.
You want to quit,
whether writing or men,
but no matter how many "ends"
you start again.
Life's not meant to be still —
move, dream,
win or lose,

we do it again

and again.

Drifter

I open the door
breathe in fresh spring air
of a new day —
My day
to take as I please.

Pack secured to bike,
six string on my back
no school, no job
just me and the open road.
Going nowhere and anywhere,
a trip to find myself.

Stop on a whim —
barter for a bed or
play for my supper,
new faces and places
shape my music.

Each day a new adventure.

I was Born in Autumn

The trees show not signs of death,
their leaves turn vivid colors,
merely a sunset of reds, yellows, orange,
a transformation

Laughter warms the chill air
as feet kick and crunch the vibrant piles

With a toss of the wind,
leaves dance down the street with joy,
until exhausted they huddle in gutters, near fences

Gardens celebrate life,
grace our tables with their bounty
Family overflows living spaces
homes rich with fall aroma
of spice and the crackle of a fire

The Quiet Poetry of Pink

cherry blossoms
painted nails, pony tails
sweet sixteen, prom dresses
childhood crushes
giggles, contagious and intoxicating
fruit dipped in whipped cream
ballet dancer, delicate yet strong
lotion seeps into skin
smooth pebbles from a stream
scent of rose petals
a blessing of unicorns

Reunion

Over food and games
Siblings catch up on news,
their familiar chatter
carries down the hall...

I smile,
comforted by their nearness,
content for the moment
to reunite with another friend —

Kick off my shoes, sit at the bench,
toes hug the familiar curve
of the pedal pressed beneath my foot,
ivory beneath my fingers.

My hands fall into patterns
despite months of time apart —
All else fades away
as I embrace the music.

Release

Rootsong

my toes
dig into grass
as I spin
leaves dance around me
like fairies

Aloft

Fairy
wings tremble
with wind's joy,
Dance in the sky —
Adventure

Druid Ring

within circle of stones
hooded figures link hands
feet bare to connect
to the earth

voices join in song
as the sun
touches the mountain

they witness the night
a bonfire lit to keep darkness at bay
until the sun's return

each member steps forward
casts off that which holds them back
burns it in the flames

death and rebirth
a new year begins —
honor the cycle

Moon's Song to Earth

Only you and I,
in our daily dance through stars,
can help the sun rise.

Each coming morning,
as our children wake to toil,
I rest in your arms.

If we don't keep on —
as we have for all known time —
our loyal cycle,

the sun would know.
In despair
it may drench itself,

the light in the sky
and the magic in this world
snuffed out in sorrow.

The Mother

Endlessly bright, fervently constant
A finite expression of the Heavens
The Mother of life itself
A beacon of Hope in the darkness
Her dance too passionate for mortal eyes
She fears her demise will end us all
She gives of herself so we may live
Yearning to see Eternity

Green Unfurls

aroma of fresh-cut grass
stretching yoga poses
fresh air after smog
surprise touch of a frog, smooth not slimy
scalp massage of green apple shampoo
the taste of kiwi
mint ice-cream
smack, run, cheer, baseball
the snap of green beans
ruins, hidden in moss and vines
willow leaves, dripping, waving

Lunar Pull

The moon begins to dance —
Tides swoon for its romance.

the dance continues

Publication Notes

Earlier versions of "Moon's Song to Earth," "Courtship Song," and "Druid Ring" also appear in Doorways to Enchantment.

About the Author

Mary W. Jensen lives in Utah with her husband and son. The middle of nine children, she learned early to find stillness inside sound, and to shape chaos into story.

She is the author of The Briarbook Lane Poetry Collection, lyrical works rooted in light and shadow. She also writes fairy-tale fantasy set in the world of Tessagonia, where grief, wonder, and quiet magic give rise to enduring hope.

When she isn't writing, she is usually reading, wandering libraries, or listening for the next rhythm that wants to be followed.

She publishes under Briarbook Lane Press.

BriarbookLane.com

The doorway is always open.

Scan to continue your journey at BriarbookLane.com.

Also by Mary W. Jensen

Tales of Tessagonia Series

The Blazing Princess

Mirror

The Princess Test

Venom and Shadow

The Gloaming Realm

The Moon Prince

Jack and the Midnight Cloak

The Drowned Song

The Unwelcome Guest

Fatinah and the Ghost Ship

Poetry

Chiaroscuro

Doorways to Enchantment

www.ingramcontent.com/pod-product-compliance
Lightning Source LLC
Chambersburg PA
CBHW020745220726
48569CB00036B/395
* 9 7 8 1 7 3 7 6 4 3 7 4 6 *